CROP SPRAYERS

By S. M. Maimone

Gareth Stevens
PUBLISHING

Please visit our website, www.garethstevens.com. For a free color catalog of all our high-quality books, call toll free 1-800-542-2595 or fax 1-877-542-2596.

Library of Congress Cataloging-in-Publication Data

Names: Maimone, Sofia Z., author.
Title: Crop sprayers / S. M. Maimone.
Description: New York : Gareth Stevens Publishing, [2017] | Series: Fantastic
  farm machines | Includes bibliographical references and index.
Identifiers: LCCN 2015045639 | ISBN 9781482445886 (pbk.) | ISBN 9781482445817
(library bound) | ISBN 9781482445695 (6 pack)
Subjects: LCSH: Agricultural machinery–Juvenile literature. | Spraying and
  dusting in agriculture–Juvenile literature.
Classification: LCC SB953 .M27 2017 | DDC 631.3–dc23
LC record available at http://lccn.loc.gov/2015045639

Published in 2017 by
Gareth Stevens Publishing
111 East 14th Street, Suite 349
New York, NY 10003

Designer: Sarah Liddell
Editor: Therese Shea

Photo credits: Cover, p. 1 Fotokostic/Shutterstock.com; spread background texture
used throughout LongQuattro/Shutterstock.com; p. 5 stoonn/Shutterstock.com;
p. 7 Lost Mountain Studio/Shutterstock.com; p. 9 Maksud/Shutterstock.com;
p. 11 ittipon/Shutterstock.com; p. 13 (trailed) EMJAY SMITH/Shutterstock.com;
p. 13 (mounted) Patrycja Zadros/Shutterstock.com; p. 15 Stockr/Shutterstock.com;
p. 17 oticki/Shutterstock.com; p. 19 Federico Rostagno/Shutterstock.com;
p. 21 Carolina K. Smith MD/Shutterstock.com.

Printed in the United States of America

CPSIA compliance information: Batch #CS16GS: For further information contact Gareth Stevens, New York, New York at 1-800-542-2595.

CONTENTS

Boldface words appear in the glossary.

What Crops Need

Most plants need soil, sunlight, and water. But farmers often need other things to keep their crops healthy, such as **fertilizers**. Spreading fertilizers and other things on crops can be a big job. That's why farmers need some big machines.

Pesky Pests and Weeds

Some farmers have a hard time keeping pests from eating crops. For example, grasshoppers eat wheat and **aphids** eat corn. So farmers may use **chemicals** called pesticides to kill pests before they can harm their crops.

7

Weeds are another problem. They take up space and may use **nutrients** in soil that crops need. Weeds can be pulled out, but it takes a lot of time to do that on large farms. So farmers may use chemicals called **herbicides** (UHR-buh-sydz).

Time to Spray

How do farmers get fertilizers, pesticides, or herbicides to their crops? On small farms, farmers might carry a **tank** full of the chemicals. The tank is connected to a spray gun that spreads the chemicals over the crops.

Trailed or Mounted

Farmers on big farms often use large machines called crop sprayers when they need to treat their crops. Some crop sprayers are connected to the back of tractors. They're called trailed or mounted sprayers.

trailed sprayer

mounted sprayer

13

Self-Propelled

Some crop sprayers are self-propelled. That means they aren't pulled by a tractor. They have their own engine that moves them. Some of the largest crop sprayers are self-propelled. They can hold a lot of chemicals and spray a large area quickly.

15

In Action

Crop sprayers have a tank that contains chemicals. They also have a wide **boom**, which covers a lot of field. A pump pushes the chemicals from the tank through pipes that run along the boom. **Nozzles** on the boom spray the chemicals.

boom

tank

nozzles

17

Farmers drive crop sprayers through the field. They go up and down the rows until all the crops are sprayed. Some booms are as wide as 150 feet (46 m), so the job goes quickly.

From Above

Some farms use planes to spray their crops. This is called **aerial** application or crop-dusting. Some of these planes don't have pilots in them. They're controlled by computers! Which kind of crop sprayer would you use on a farm? Why?

GLOSSARY

aerial: done by aircraft

aphid: a very small bug that harms plants

boom: a long pole or arm

chemical: matter that can be mixed with other matter to cause changes

fertilizer: something that makes soil better for growing crops and other plants

herbicide: a chemical used to destroy plants or stop plant growth

nozzle: a short tube on the end of a hose or pipe to control the way a liquid flows out

nutrient: something a living thing needs to grow and stay alive

tank: an object that holds liquid or gas

FOR MORE INFORMATION

BOOKS

Dickmann, Nancy. *Food from Farms*. Chicago, IL: Heinemann Library, 2011.

Peppas, Lynn. *Vehicles on the Farm*. New York, NY: Crabtree Publishing, 2011.

Veitch, Catherine. *Farms Around the World*. Chicago, IL: Heinemann Library, 2012.

WEBSITES

Agriculture
www.neok12.com/Agriculture.htm
Lots of videos about farming can be found on this site.

Kids Farm
www.kidsfarm.com
This site has many links, puzzles, and games that teach about farms.

INDEX